D1400889

BATTY
About
TEXAS

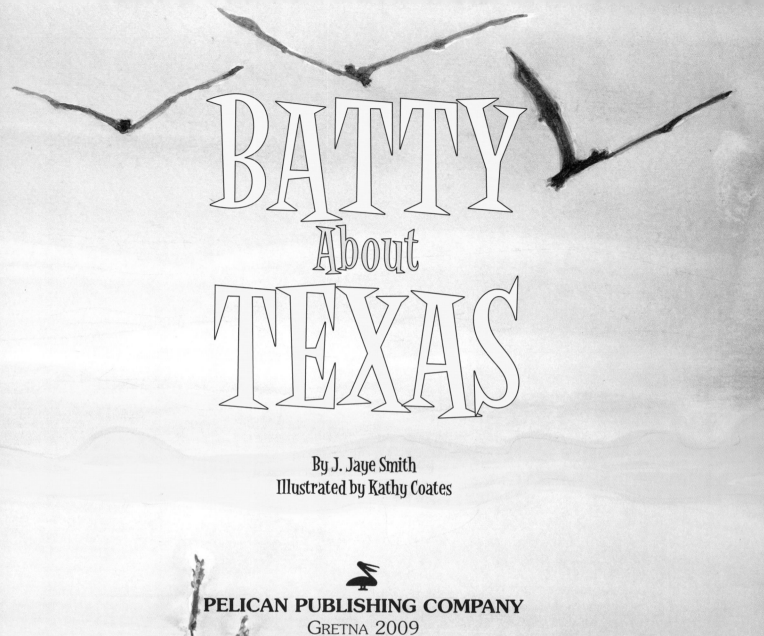

BATTY About TEXAS

By J. Jaye Smith

Illustrated by Kathy Coates

PELICAN PUBLISHING COMPANY

GRETNA 2009

To Ms. Nina Kooij, Dr. Milburn Calhoun, and
Dr. William Getman. Thank you, thank you, thank you!—J. J. S.

The word "Pelican" and the depiction of a pelican are trademarks
of Pelican Publishing Company, Inc., and are registered in the
U.S. Patent and Trademark Office.

Library of Congress Cataloging-in-Publication Data

Smith, J. Jaye.
  Batty about Texas / by J. Jaye Smith ; illustrated by Kathy Coates.
    p. cm.
  ISBN 978-1-58980-582-8 (hardcover : alk. paper) 1. Tadarida brasiliensis—Texas—Juvenile literature. 2. Tadarida brasiliensis—Juvenile literature. I. Coates, Kathy, 1950-, ill. II. Title.
  QL737.C54S55 2008
  599.409764—dc22

                                    2008006024

Printed in Singapore

Published by Pelican Publishing Company, Inc.
1000 Burmaster Street, Gretna, Louisiana 70053

Batty About Texas

Hola! Hello! I am Bo, a Mexican free-tailed bat. You may think that means I only live in Mexico, but in fact, I was born in the great state of Texas.

Each spring, millions of Mexican free-tailed bats migrate from Mexico to Texas. New pups are born there each summer. It's only in late fall, when the air cools, that we return to Mexico.

Bat fact: Baby bats are called pups.

Some say everything is bigger and better in Texas. This is indeed true for bats! Texas has thirty-two different kinds of bats, more than any other state. But wait . . . that's not all! The biggest bat colony on earth can be found in Texas too. Can you believe it?

It's true! Near San Antonio, over 20 million Mexican free-tailed bats roost in a place called Bracken Cave. Imagine. There are almost as many bats in one cave as there are people in the entire state of Texas. Texas is a big state—the second largest in the U.S.A.!

Bat fact: A group of bats, all living together, is called a colony.

Still, Mexican free-tailed bats don't just live in caves. We live in cities too. As many as 1.5 million live in downtown Austin, underneath the Congress Avenue Bridge. This is the largest urban bat colony in North America.

Fortunately, people in Austin like having bats around. Bat viewing at the bridge has become one of the state capital's most popular tourist activities. The city even placed an enormous sculpture there in our honor.

We're in the cities and in the country. We're deep in caves and under bridges. Bats live all across Texas! So I've told you about where I live. Now let me tell you more about who I am and what I do!

For starters, I am a mammal. You are a mammal too! Think about it like this: a mammal is an animal that has warm blood, grows some kind of hair, and gives birth to live babies. We have this in common.

Bat fact: About one of every four mammals on earth is a bat.

However, I am not like you in one big way. I can *fly!* I am not a bird, but I can fly very high and very fast. Really!

Bat fact: Bats are the only mammals that can truly fly.

A Mexican free-tailed bat can fly up to two miles high in the sky! That's higher than even the tallest building in the world. And I can fly about as fast as your car drives on the highway. My speed makes me one of the quickest bats around.

Do you know another way we're different? I am nocturnal. You are diurnal. This means you are active during the day and I am active at night! And when you sleep, you probably lie out flat, but I don't. Bats sleep while hanging upside down!

Just like you, I need to eat and drink every day. This is why Mexican free-tailed bats usually live near water. Not only do we drink it, but water attracts our favorite food: flying insects! That's right. I eat bugs!

Bat fact: Bats are not "blind," but they use a special sense called echolocation to help them hunt at night. When the bat makes a noise, it travels. If the sound meets something in its path, it bounces off and returns to the bat. This helps the bat find its way.

Each dusk, we all awake at once. Together, we speed into the darkening sky like one twisting tornado. *Zoom!* The chase for breakfast is on. In a single night, one bat may eat close to its own weight in bugs.

That's incredible! In case you missed it, let me explain. This would be something like a typical five-year-old human eating 100 bananas in one day. Can you imagine how that would feel?

Luckily for you, the mosquito is one of the bugs I like to eat. Remember: the more I eat, the fewer there are to bite you!

We also eat moths, beetles, and other bugs that are harmful to plants. With our help, Texas farmers need fewer chemical pesticides to protect their growing crops. And don't forget, fewer chemicals makes Texas a healthier place for everyone.

As they say, what goes in must come out. While bats don't use bathrooms, we do make waste. Our "poop" is called guano, and it is actually useful. People have put it into products such as cleaners, medicines, and fertilizers.

That leads me to yet another reason why bats are great for Texas! With so many of us about, we make enough waste to fertilize countless acres of Texas crops (saving farmers millions of dollars each year).

At 100 million and counting, more bats live in Texas than in any other state. For this reason alone, I think Texas can proudly say it's the battiest state in the U.S.A.

And while far more bats than people live in Texas, most people will never see one of us up close. Yet we are always doing our part to make Texas a cleaner, safer, and healthier place for all living creatures.

Well, I guess that's it for now. I so enjoyed sharing my story with you. I hope you won't forget about me and all of my bat family. I am Bo and now you know why I am absolutely batty about Texas. *Adios!* Goodbye!

Author's Note

The Mexican free-tailed bat colonies of Texas are mainly maternity colonies. This means most of the bats are females that migrate from Mexico to Texas, where one female adult may have only one pup each year. Some colonies in east Texas, however, are known to stay year round.

All population numbers mentioned here are peak estimations. A Mexican free-tailed bat's body is about three and a half inches long. The bat is sometimes enlarged here to better show its detail.

To learn more, visit Bat Conservation International at batcon.org.